MASTER YOUR BUDGE

Simple Strategies for Managing
Your Personal Finances

C YK

CONTENTS

Title Page
Introduction 1
Chapter 1: The Basics of Financial Management 3
Chapter 2: How to Create a Realistic Budget 17
Chapter 3: Tracking Expenses and Income 31
Chapter 4: Tools and Applications for Money Management 47
Chapter 5: Adopting Positive Financial Behavior 64
Conclusion 75

INTRODUCTION

Personal financial management is often perceived as an intimidating and complex task, reserved for experts or people with advanced knowledge in economics. Yet, it is an essential skill within everyone's reach that can transform our daily lives and help us achieve our goals, whether it's buying a house, financing our children's education, or simply living more serenely. This guide is designed to accompany you step by step in learning and mastering your personal finances. It is intended for both beginners and those who already have some knowledge but wish to deepen certain aspects of financial management. We will start by exploring the basics of financial management to establish solid foundations. Then, we will see how to create a realistic budget, an essential first step towards controlled financial management. It is not enough to create a budget; you also need to learn to follow it scrupulously. You will discover the best methods for tracking your expenses and income. Finally, we will discuss modern tools and applications that can make your life easier because, although the principles of financial management have not changed, the means have considerably modernized. This guide is intended to be practical and accessible. You will find not only theoretical explanations but also concrete examples, case studies, and practical advice to help you immediately apply what you have learned. Our goal is to demystify personal financial management and show you that anyone can take control of their finances and improve their financial situation. One notable addition to this guide is the inclusion of a chapter dedicated to financial behavior, essential for mastering and respecting your budget. Understanding behavioral biases and adopting positive financial habits will allow you to maintain a balanced budget and make more informed financial decisions. By taking control of your finances, you will open the door to a more serene and fulfilling life. Ready to start this journey towards better resource management? Take a deep breath, arm yourself with patience and determination, and let's embark together on this exciting adventure!

CHAPTER 1: THE BASICS OF FINANCIAL MANAGEMENT

1.1 Introduction to Financial Management

Personal financial management is an essential skill that greatly influences our quality of life and well-being. It involves organizing, planning, and managing our financial resources to make informed decisions and live in financial security.

Understanding financial management starts with recognizing the importance of order in our finances. By implementing structured and thoughtful practices, we can not only avoid daily financial hassles but also anticipate and plan for the future. Whether your goal is to save for an important purchase, reduce your debts, or simply better control your spending, effective financial management is key.

At the heart of financial management are simple but powerful concepts: income, expenses, savings, and investment. Knowing when and how to balance these elements is fundamental. Financial management is not just about knowing how much we earn or spend each month; it also encompasses how we plan and act to achieve our short- and long-term goals.

But why focus on personal financial management? Because, quite simply, it allows us to live the life we want. It offers us the freedom to make decisions without constantly being stressed by financial constraints. It also allows us to build a solid future, whether for ourselves or for our loved ones.

Moreover, being in control of your personal finances brings a sense of satisfaction and accomplishment. As you learn the basics of financial management, you will discover how small daily actions can lead to significant improvements in your long-term financial situation.

That is why this first chapter will lay the essential foundations of personal financial management. We will explore the fundamental concepts and principles that will guide you throughout this journey. You will also learn how to set financial goals that you can achieve through meticulous planning and rigorous discipline.

Take this introduction as a first step towards complete mastery of your finances. By understanding and applying the basics presented, you will be better prepared to make informed decisions and build the financial security you deserve.

1.2 Key Definitions and Fundamental Concepts

Before diving into the details of personal financial management, it is important to understand a few key definitions and fundamental concepts. These notions will serve as a basis for all the financial steps and decisions you undertake.

Income:

Income constitutes all the financial resources you receive over a given period, usually monthly. This includes your salary, possibly additional income such as bonuses, allowances, investment interests, or even passive income like rent. Understanding your different sources of income is essential for effective financial management.

Expenses:

Expenses represent the money you use to cover your needs and desires. They are mainly divided into two categories: fixed expenses and variable expenses. Fixed expenses include rent, loans, insurance, while variable expenses cover groceries, entertainment, clothing, etc. Tracking and identifying your types of expenses helps determine where adjustments can be made.

Savings:

Savings is a part of your income that you set aside with the intention of using it later. It can be intended for specific short-term goals (vacations, purchase of a good) or long-term goals (retirement, emergency fund). Regular savings, even small amounts, can lead to increased financial security and the ability to face unexpected events.

Investment:

Investing involves using part of your income or savings to acquire financial assets (stocks, bonds, real estate, etc.) in the hope of generating a return on investment in the future. Investments usually involve some risk but are also a means of growing your money faster than if you just left it in a savings account.

Debt:

A debt is a sum of money you have borrowed and must repay, often with interest. Debts can be useful and necessary for significant expenses such as buying a house or financing education, but prudent management is crucial to avoid the pitfalls of excessive indebtedness.

Cash Flow:

Cash flow represents the flow of money coming in and out of your personal finances. A positive cash flow means your income exceeds your expenses, while a negative cash flow points to potential problems requiring budget adjustments.

Budget:

A budget is a detailed plan of your income and expenses over a given period. It allows you to allocate your resources optimally to achieve your financial goals and maintain control over your finances. Budgeting is an indispensable management tool that helps you avoid overspending and promote savings.

Financial Goals:

Financial goals are the targets you set for the use of your money. They can include short-term goals like saving for a vacation or long-term goals like preparing for retirement. Clearly defining your goals helps you stay focused and motivated in your financial management efforts.

By mastering these essential concepts, you will lay the solid foundations necessary for effectively managing your finances and making informed decisions. These principles will guide you throughout your journey towards better personal financial management.

1.3 Basic Principles of Financial Management

Personal financial management is based on several basic principles that every individual should integrate into their financial routine. These principles serve as guides for a healthy and effective management of your resources, allowing you to maintain stability and achieve your financial goals.

1. **Live Below Your Means:**

One of the most fundamental principles of financial management is to spend less than you earn. This involves discipline and awareness of your consumption habits. By adopting this principle, you create a financial surplus that you can use to save or invest, thus supporting your long-term financial goals.

2. **Save Regularly:**

Saving should be a priority in your monthly budget. The amount saved can vary depending on your income and expenses, but the essential thing is to do it regularly. Automatic saving, where a portion of your income is directly transferred to a savings account, can facilitate this habit.

3. **Avoid Unnecessary Debts:**

Although some debts may be necessary, such as a mortgage, it is crucial to avoid superfluous debts that can quickly accumulate and lead to a precarious financial situation. Opt for cash purchases whenever possible and be cautious with credit card use.

4. **Plan for Emergencies:**

Having an emergency fund is indispensable for facing unexpected expenses without disrupting your budget or causing additional indebtedness. A good emergency fund should cover at least three to six months of your current expenses.

5. **Invest in Your Future:**

Saving alone may not be enough to secure your financial future. Wisely chosen investments, whether in stocks, bonds, or real estate, can increase your resources in the long term. Diversifying your investments is also recommended to reduce risks.

6. Track and Adjust Your Financial Plan:

Effective financial management requires continuous monitoring of your income and expenses. By regularly tracking your budget and adjusting according to new realities in your life (income increase, spending changes, new goals), you stay in control of your financial situation.

7. Set Clear Financial Goals:

Clear and defined goals give you direction and motivation to manage your finances. These goals should be specific, measurable, achievable, relevant, and time-bound (SMART). Whether for buying a house, preparing for retirement, or financing your children's education, well-defined goals facilitate financial planning.

8. Educate and Inform Yourself:

Financial management is not a static skill; it evolves with time and circumstances. Investing in your own financial education through books, courses, specialized blogs, or financial advisors will help you stay informed and constantly improve your financial strategies.

By applying these basic principles, you lay the foundations for solid financial management. These principles are the pillars on which effective money management rests, protecting you from financial uncertainties and helping you achieve your economic ambitions.

1.4 Setting Financial Goals: Short Term vs Long Term

Setting financial goals is a crucial step in managing your personal finances. It provides a clear and motivating direction for your financial efforts. To be effective, these goals must be categorized according to their timeframe: short term, medium term, and long term.

Short-Term Goals:

Short-term financial goals are those you want to achieve in a relatively short period, generally less than a year. They can include projects like building an emergency fund, paying off a credit card debt, saving for a vacation, or buying a new household appliance.

These goals require quick planning and execution. They often necessitate immediate adjustments in your budget to save the necessary amount within the allotted time. Establishing these goals gives you quick wins, reinforcing your motivation and saving habits.

Medium-Term Goals:

Medium-term financial goals usually cover a period of one to five years. They include more ambitious projects like saving for a car, preparing an education fund for your children, or planning a major home renovation.

These goals require a more elaborate financial strategy and continuous discipline. You can combine saving techniques and low-risk investments to achieve these goals. Midway through the timeframe, it may be useful to reassess your progress and adjust your plan if necessary.

Long-Term Goals:

Long-term goals extend over a period of five years or more. They include major projects like buying a house, preparing for retirement, or building a robust investment portfolio.

These goals require rigorous planning and often a combination of saving and long-term investing. Stocks, bonds, and real estate are examples of investments suitable for achieving long-term goals. It is crucial to periodically reassess your progress and diversify your investments to minimize risks and maximize returns.

SMART: Define Your Goals

To maximize your chances of success, use the SMART method to define your financial goals. They should be Specific (clearly defined), Measurable (quantifiable), Achievable (realistic), Relevant (meaningful), and Time-bound (with a precise deadline).

Alignment with Your Financial Situation:

Ensure that your financial goals match your current and anticipated future situation. For example, if you foresee a career change, adjust your financial goals accordingly. An honest assessment of your income, expenses, and priorities will help you set realistic and achievable goals.

Planning and Reevaluation:

Once you have set your goals, establish a detailed action plan for each of them. This includes specific steps and the amount to save or invest regularly. Remember to reassess your goals regularly to ensure they remain relevant and aligned with your aspirations and life conditions.

By setting well-defined financial goals and categorizing them according to their timeframe, you lay the foundations for proactive financial management oriented towards achieving your ambitions. These goals serve as a compass, guiding your daily financial decisions and giving you the means to build a financially secure future.

1.5 The Importance of Saving and Investing

Saving and investing are essential pillars of personal financial management. They play complementary roles in building a stable and prosperous financial future. Understanding their importance and knowing how to differentiate them is crucial for implementing an effective financial strategy.

Saving: Security for the Future

Saving involves setting aside a portion of your income for future needs. It is a fundamental component of any prudent financial management, as it allows you to create an emergency fund, plan for significant expenses, and protect yourself against financial surprises.

Why Save?

- **Financial Security:** An emergency fund serves as a financial cushion that can help you face unexpected situations such as job loss, medical expenses, or urgent repairs.
- **Short- and Medium-Term Goals:** Saving allows you to plan and finance specific projects like vacations, purchasing a new car, or home renovations without resorting to debt.
- **Cash Management:** It offers financial flexibility by ensuring you always have available liquidity to cover your basic needs and desires.

How to Maximize Your Savings?

- **Automation:** Set up automatic transfers from your current account to your savings account to ensure regularity.
- **Regular Evaluation:** Regularly review your budget and adjust your savings contributions according to your goals and financial situation.

Investing: Growing Your Money

Investing, on the other hand, aims to use part of your capital to generate a return over a given period. Unlike saving, which is often low-risk and easily accessible, investing involves risks but offers significant growth opportunities.

Why Invest?

- **Capital Growth:** Investments can offer higher returns than traditional savings accounts, thus increasing the value of your money over time.
- **Retirement Preparation:** Investing in retirement plans or diversified investment portfolios allows you to build significant capital for your post-work years.
- **Achieving Long-Term Goals:** Long-term investments in stocks, bonds, or real estate can help you achieve major financial goals like buying property or funding your children's education.

Effective Investment Strategies:

- **Diversification:** Spread your investments across different asset classes to minimize risks (stocks, bonds, real estate, etc.).
- **Research and Education:** Inform yourself about different investment options and consult financial experts to develop a strategy tailored to your goals and risk tolerance.

Combining Saving and Investing

For optimal financial management, saving and investing should work together. Saving provides the security needed for your immediate and unexpected needs, while investing helps grow your wealth and achieve long-term financial goals.

Balanced Plan:

- **Short Term:** Prioritize creating an emergency fund and saving for short-term goals.
- **Long Term:** Allocate part of your finances to

investments suited to your goals and risk tolerance.

In summary, saving and investing are key steps to ensuring healthy financial management. While saving protects you against the unexpected and immediate needs, investing helps build a solid and prosperous financial future. By integrating these practices into your financial routine, you make informed decisions that will contribute to your long-term financial stability and growth.

1.6 Understanding and Managing Debt

Debts are an integral part of many people's financial lives. Well understood and well managed, they can be used as levers to achieve important financial goals. However, poorly managed, they can quickly become a burden, delaying the achievement of your goals and compromising your financial security. The key lies in a thorough understanding of debts and effective methods to manage them.

Types of Debt:

It is essential to distinguish between different types of debt for better management:

- **Productive Debts:** These are debts incurred for investments that increase your long-term asset value, such as mortgages or student loans. These debts are generally considered "good" because they contribute to the growth of your assets or income potential.
- **Non-Productive Debts:** These are debts incurred for current expenses or consumer goods purchases that do not generate future income, such as credit card debts or personal loans. These debts should be managed with caution as they can quickly accumulate and become costly.

Why Manage Your Debts?

Prudent debt management is crucial to maintaining your financial health. Uncontrolled debts can lead to high interest rates, late fees, and even repercussions on your credit score. However, strategic debt management can enhance your purchasing power and support your investment projects.

Debt Management Strategies:

1. **Create a Repayment Plan:**
    - **Inventory Your Debts:** List all your debts with their amounts,

interest rates, and due dates.
- **Prioritize Repayments:** Focus first on debts with the highest interest rates. Another approach is the "snowball" method, where you repay the smallest debts first to gain a sense of accomplishment and increased motivation.

2. **Negotiate with Your Creditors:**
- If you encounter difficulties in repayment, contact your creditors to negotiate more favorable repayment terms. This may include a reduced interest rate, an extension of the repayment period, or an adjusted payment plan.

3. **Consolidate Your Debts:**
- Consolidating multiple debts into a single debt at a lower interest rate can simplify management and reduce the overall cost of interest. However, it is crucial to understand the consolidation terms to avoid unnecessarily extending the repayment period.

4. **Follow Your Budget:**
- Maintaining a strict budget is important to adequately allocate a portion of your income to debt repayment while covering your current expenses. Use financial tracking tools to stay aligned with your repayment goals.

5. **Avoid Accumulating New Debts:**
- Adopt responsible consumption habits and avoid using credit for non-essential purchases. If possible, pay in cash or by debit to maintain control over your expenses.

6. **Educate Yourself:**
- Inform yourself about the legal and financial implications of your debts. Understanding loan contracts, interest rates, and late penalties will prevent unpleasant surprises and costly mistakes.

The Impact of Debt Management on Your Financial Well-Being:

Effective debt management allows you to reduce financial stress, improve your credit score, and free up financial resources for other goals like saving and investing. It also contributes to better financial stability and an increased ability to face unexpected events.

In conclusion, although unavoidable for many, debts do not have to be a constant source of stress. With prudent management and well-thought-out strategies, you can use debts to your advantage, build a solid financial foundation, and progress towards your economic goals in a sustained and reliable manner.

CHAPTER 2: HOW TO CREATE A REALISTIC BUDGET

After laying the foundations of financial management, it is time to move to the next step: creating a realistic budget. This chapter will guide you through the necessary steps to create a budget that accurately reflects your income and expenses, helping you better control your finances and achieve your financial goals.

2.1 Importance of Budgeting

Creating a budget is a crucial step in personal financial management. A clear and well-structured budget allows you to take control of your finances, plan your spending, and achieve your financial goals. It provides a framework to organize your resources and ensures the judicious use of your income.

Financial Control:

A budget allows you to know exactly where your money goes each month. By having a clear view of your financial inflows and outflows, you can identify and adjust superfluous spending habits. This helps you avoid financial overruns and maintain a balance between your income and expenses.

Reducing Financial Stress:

By establishing a budget, you can anticipate and plan your expenses, thereby reducing the uncertainty and stress associated with managing personal finances. A budget gives you peace of mind by ensuring that all your financial obligations, such as rent and bills, will be covered.

Achieving Financial Goals:

A well-crafted budget helps you allocate specific resources for your financial goals. Whether you want to save for a trip, repay a debt, or invest, a budget allows you to plan these goals realistically and track your progress.

Preparing for Unexpected Expenses:

Having a budget also enables you to set aside funds for unexpected expenses. By reserving part of your income for an emergency fund, you will be better prepared to handle financial surprises without compromising your other financial goals.

Optimizing Resources:

With a budget, you can optimize the use of your financial resources. Instead of guessing how much you can spend, you have clear guidelines that help you maximize every euro earned. This is crucial to avoid waste and to invest intelligently.

Strengthening Financial Discipline:

Creating and following a budget requires discipline but brings many long-term benefits. This discipline translates into better management of spending habits, allowing you to make more prudent and informed financial choices.

In summary, the importance of a budget cannot be underestimated. It is the basic tool that supports all your financial decisions and ensures the stability and growth of your financial situation. A well-thought-out and regularly updated budget is key to achieving your financial goals and living more serenely and structured.

2.2 Steps to Create a Budget

Creating a realistic and effective budget involves following several key steps. These steps will guide you in organizing your finances, tracking your spending, and maximizing your saving and investment potential.

1. **Gather Financial Information:**

Start by compiling all information about your income and expenses. This includes:
- **Income:** Salary, additional income, passive income (rent, interest), allowances, etc.
- **Fixed Expenses:** Rent or mortgage, insurance, subscriptions, loan payments.
- **Variable Expenses:** Groceries, transportation, entertainment, clothing.
- **Occasional Expenses:** Repairs, gifts, medical expenses.

2. **Calculate Income and Expenses:**

Determine your total monthly income by adding all income sources. Likewise, add up your fixed, variable, and occasional expenses to get your total monthly expenses. This step gives you an accurate overview of your financial situation.

3. **Set Budget Categories:**

Divide your expenses into distinct categories for better management. Categories can include:
- **Necessities:** Rent/mortgage, food, transportation, utilities.
- **Savings and Investment:** Emergency fund, retirement savings, various investments.
- **Wants:** Entertainment, outings, travel, shopping.

This segmentation helps identify areas where adjustments can be made to optimize spending.

4. **Set Spending Limits:**

Assign a specific amount to each spending category based on

your priorities and financial goals. Ensure that the total of all categories does not exceed your available monthly income. This step helps you stay within your budget limits.

5. **Implement the Budget:**

Create a document or use a financial management app to structure your budget. Note the amounts allocated to each category and the review dates. This gives you a clear roadmap to track your spending and progress.

6. **Track Spending:**

Record all your daily expenses and allocate them to the appropriate categories. This can be done manually in a journal, via a spreadsheet, or using a spending tracking app. Regular tracking is essential to stay aligned with your budget and quickly identify discrepancies.

7. **Reevaluate and Adjust:**

At the end of each month, compare your actual spending to the planned budget. Analyze discrepancies to understand where adjustments are needed. This may involve reducing certain categories or increasing others based on your needs and priorities.

8. **Periodic Review:**

A budget is not static; it must evolve with your financial situation. Review your budget periodically—at least every six months—to adjust amounts based on changes in your income, expenses, or financial goals.

By following these steps, you will create a budget that is not only realistic but also flexible, reflecting your current needs and helping to plan for the future. Well-executed, a budget acts as a financial compass, guiding your economic decisions and ensuring your progress towards better stability and financial prosperity.

2.3 Budgeting Methods

There are several budgeting methods you can adopt depending on your preferences, financial situation, and goals. Each of these methods has its advantages and can be adapted to different financial management styles.

The 50/30/20 Method:

This method divides your after-tax income into three major categories:

- **50% for Necessities:** These are essential expenses like housing, food, utilities, and transportation.
- **30% for Wants:** These include entertainment, outings, shopping, and other personal pleasures.
- **20% for Savings and Debt Repayment:** Includes savings for emergencies, investments, and debt repayment.

This simple and flexible method facilitates financial management while ensuring a balance between needs, wants, and savings.

The Zero-Based Budgeting Method:

Zero-based budgeting means allocating every euro you earn to a specific category until you have "zero" euros left at the end of the month. This includes all expenses, savings, and debt repayment. Every euro has a purpose:

Income - Expenses - Savings = Zero

This method requires meticulous planning and rigorous tracking, but it maximizes the efficiency of every euro earned.

The Envelope Budgeting Method:

This method involves allocating cash to different envelopes representing spending categories like groceries, entertainment, or clothing. Once the money in an envelope is exhausted, no further spending can be made in that category until the next month:

- **Physical or Digital Envelopes:** Apps can replace physical envelopes for those who prefer digital.

This method helps limit impulsive spending and promotes strict spending discipline.

The Pay-Yourself-First Method:

This method prioritizes savings before expenses. You first allocate a portion of your income to your savings and investments, then use the rest for your necessary and discretionary expenses:

- **Automatic Savings and Investments:** Automate these transfers to ensure consistency.
- **Remaining for Expenses:** The rest of your income is used for your daily life expenses.

This method encourages effective saving discipline and ensures that savings are not left until the end of the month, after expenses.

The Traditional Budgeting Method:

Here, you set a fixed amount for each spending category at the beginning of the month. This method is the most detailed and requires in-depth planning of each expense:

- **Detailed Categorization:** Food, housing, transportation, savings, entertainment, etc.
- **Rigorous Tracking:** Regular comparison of actual expenses with budgeted amounts.

This method is particularly suited to those who like precision and detailed control over their finances.

The Rollover Budgeting Method:

With this method, funds not spent in a category at the end of the month are carried over to the next month. This creates financial flexibility and allows saving in certain categories to prepare for larger future expenses:

- **Positive Rollover:** Unspent this month can be used later.
- **Negative Rollover:** Overages covered by future savings transfers.

The Needs vs. Wants Budgeting Method:

This method involves rigorously distinguishing between needs and wants. By prioritizing your needs and then allocating a portion of your income to wants, you ensure that essential expenses are always covered first.

Each method presents specific advantages and can be chosen based on your financial habits and long-term goals. The important thing is to find a method that fits your lifestyle and helps you achieve your financial goals rigorously and practically.

2.4 Practical Budget Table Example

To illustrate how to create a budget, we will present a practical example of a monthly budget table. This table will allow you to visualize how to organize your income and expenses to maximize your financial efficiency.

Monthly Budget Table

Income:

Category	Amount (€)
Main Salary	2500
Additional Income	500
Passive Income	200
Total Income	**3200**

Expenses:

Fixed Expenses:

Category	Amount (€)
Rent/Mortgage	800
Home Insurance	50
Car Insurance	70
Utilities	150
Phone/Internet	60
Student Loans	200
Total Fixed Expenses	**1330**

Variable Expenses:

Category	Amount (€)
Groceries	300
Transportation (gas, etc.)	100
Entertainment	150
Restaurants	100
Clothing	100
Health and Wellness	50

Miscellaneous	100
Total Variable Expenses	900

Occasional Expenses:

Category	Amount (€)
Car Repairs	100
Gifts	50
Medical Expenses	50
Total Occasional Expenses	200

Savings and Investments:

Category	Amount (€)
Emergency Fund	200
Retirement Savings	200
Investments	200
Total Savings and Investments	600

Summary:

Category	Amount (€)
Total Income	3200
Total Expenses	2430
Total Savings and Investments	600
Available Balance	170

Analysis of the Table:

This budget table presents a detailed breakdown of income and expenses over a month. Expenses are clearly divided into fixed, variable, and occasional for better management and adjustment. The table also highlights the importance of savings and investments by allocating a significant portion of income to these crucial categories.

Possible Adjustments:

After following this model for a few months, analyze your actual expenses compared to your planned budget. Adjust amounts based on your priorities and financial goals:

- **Increase Savings:** If you find areas where you can reduce costs, allocate these savings to your emergency fund or investments to strengthen your financial security.
- **Reduce Variable Expenses:** Identify categories where expenses often flare up, such as entertainment or dining out, and set stricter limits.

This practical budget table example offers a solid foundation for structuring and tracking your finances. By personalizing this model according to your unique situation, you will be better equipped to manage your resources and achieve your financial goals effectively.

2.5 Tracking and Adjusting Your Budget

Creating a budget is only the first step; following and regularly adjusting it is essential for effective financial management and achieving your goals. Here are the key steps to tracking and adjusting your budget.

1. **Daily and Weekly Tracking:**

To maintain control over your finances, it is crucial to track your expenses daily or, at least, weekly. This allows you to quickly identify discrepancies and take immediate corrective action:

- **Record Every Expense:** Note every expense, no matter how small, as soon as it occurs. You can use financial management apps, spreadsheets, or a notebook.
- **Classify Expenses:** Classify each expense into its respective budget categories (food, transportation, entertainment, etc.).

2. **Monthly Analysis:**

At the end of each month, compare your actual expenses to those planned in your budget. This helps you understand where you excel and where adjustments are necessary:

- **Discrepancy Report:** Identify discrepancies between budgeted and actual expenses. Note the categories where you exceeded the budget and those where you spent less than expected.
- **Performance Evaluation:** Analyze the reasons for discrepancies. Were there unexpected expenses or changes in your income? This information provides clues on financial habits to readjust.

3. **Budget Adjustment:**

Based on your monthly analysis, adjust your budget for the following month. Adjustments may include:

- **Increasing or Decreasing Allocations:** If some categories consistently exceed their budgets, you may

reevaluate these amounts. Conversely, categories where you underspend can have their allocations reduced.
- **Revising Priorities:** If your financial goals change or unforeseen events occur (new fixed expense, change in income), adapt your budget accordingly.

4. **Tools and Technologies:**

Use digital tools for precise and simplified tracking:
- **Financial Management Apps:** Apps like Mint, YNAB (You Need a Budget), and PocketGuard help automate expense tracking and provide real-time analyses.
- **Spreadsheets:** Customized spreadsheets on Excel or Google Sheets can also be used for detailed and adjustable tracking according to your needs.

5. **Monthly Budget Meeting:**

Organize a monthly "budget meeting," alone or with family if you share finances, to discuss the state of the budget. This is a dedicated time to review the past month's performance, adjust categories, and plan for the next month:
- **Discuss Successes and Challenges:** What worked well? What lessons can be learned from discrepancies?
- **Plan Adjustments:** Together, define the necessary adjustments and ensure all family members are aligned with budget goals.

6. **Flexibility and Adaptations:**

Be flexible and ready to adapt your budget based on unforeseen circumstances or changes in your personal and professional situation:
- **Income Changes:** Quickly adjust your budget in case of significant income changes to avoid deficits and reallocate resources efficiently.
- **Unexpected Events:** Be ready to review your budget in case of major unexpected expenses or changes in your financial outlook.

7. **Continuous Education:**

Keep yourself informed about best budgeting practices and

adjust your methods accordingly. Participating in financial workshops, reading specialized articles, and consulting experts can enrich your budget tracking and adjustment strategies.

By systematically following these steps, you can maintain strict control over your finances, adjust your plans according to your progress and challenges, and achieve your financial goals with greater precision and efficiency. Consistency and rigor in tracking and adjusting your budget are essential for sustainable and successful financial management.

CHAPTER 3: TRACKING EXPENSES AND INCOME

With a budget in place, it is crucial to closely monitor your expenses and income to stay on track. This chapter focuses on financial tracking techniques and tools, allowing you to analyze your spending habits, detect budget discrepancies, and adjust your plans accordingly.

3.1 Importance of Financial Tracking

Carefully tracking your finances is a fundamental aspect of personal financial management. It is not just about knowing how much money you have, but understanding how and why you spend it. This enables you to make informed decisions, prevent financial problems, and achieve your economic goals.

Financial Clarity and Transparency:

Financial tracking provides a clear and detailed view of your income and expenses. This transparency is crucial to know where your money is really going. Without precise tracking, it is easy to underestimate certain expenses, leading to significant budget discrepancies.

Prediction and Planning:

Tracking your finances allows you to forecast future cash flows. By understanding your spending and income habits, you can anticipate periods of tight cash flow and plan accordingly. This helps you avoid financial surprises and establish reserves for unexpected expenses.

Identification of Spending Habits:

Financial tracking helps you identify your spending habits. This includes categories where you spend the most, impulsive or recurring expenses, and areas where you can potentially reduce costs. Knowing these habits is the first step to making positive changes to your financial behavior.

Debt Prevention:

Regularly tracking your finances helps you avoid accumulating unnecessary debt. By keeping an eye on your expenses and credit balances, you can take corrective measures before they become problematic. This includes repaying existing debts and avoiding new ones.

Evaluation of Goal Achievement:

Tracking your finances also allows you to measure your progress towards your financial goals. Whether it's saving for a trip, buying a house, or building a retirement fund, financial tracking gives you benchmarks to assess if you are on the right track or if adjustments are needed.

Improved Decision-Making:

Having precise and up-to-date financial information improves the quality of your economic decisions. You can decide how much to save, where to invest, or whether you can afford certain expenses based on real data rather than approximations.

Stress Reduction:

Financial uncertainty is often a major source of stress. By tracking your finances, you gain control and assurance that reduce anxiety related to money matters. You know exactly where you stand, which promotes peace of mind.

Tax Optimization:

Meticulous financial tracking also facilitates tax preparation and planning. You can identify available deductions and credits, organize your financial documents, and avoid late penalties through proactive and well-informed management.

Adaptation to Changes:

Life is full of changes: job change, marriage, birth, or home purchase. By closely tracking your finances, you can quickly adjust your budget and strategies according to these new circumstances, ensuring continuous financial stability.

In conclusion, financial tracking is not a secondary task; it is an essential activity for successful financial management. By committing to rigorously tracking your income and expenses, you lay the foundation for sustainable financial stability, improve your ability to achieve your goals, and reduce stress related to economic uncertainties.

3.2 Tools for Tracking Expenses and Income

To effectively track your finances, it is essential to use appropriate tools. These tools can greatly simplify the process, provide accurate information, and help you make better financial decisions. Here is an overview of the main types of tools available for tracking expenses and income.

1. **Traditional Tools:**

Account Books: Using a notebook to record your expenses and income remains a simple and effective method. You can note each daily transaction and manually calculate the totals for different periods. This method is ideal for those who prefer a tactile and visual approach.

Excel Spreadsheets: Spreadsheets like Excel offer increased flexibility for financial tracking. You can create custom tables to record your income, expenses, and perform automatic calculations. Excel also allows you to generate charts that provide a clear overview of your financial situation.

2. **Mobile and Online Applications:**

Mint: Mint is a popular app that centralizes your bank accounts, credit cards, bills, and investments in one place. It automatically categorizes your transactions, allows you to set budgets, and offers alerts for budget overruns or upcoming bill payments.

You Need A Budget (YNAB): YNAB is an app focused on proactive income allocation. It helps users plan every dollar earned, track expenses in real time, and make informed financial decisions. YNAB also emphasizes debt management and emergency savings.

PocketGuard: PocketGuard simplifies financial tracking by connecting your bank accounts and automatically categorizing your expenses. It shows how much money you have left after covering your necessities, bills, and savings goals. It's an excellent tool to avoid overspending.

3. **Financial Management Software:**

Quicken: Quicken is a comprehensive financial management software that offers advanced features for expense tracking, budgeting, and investment management. It allows you to monitor your finances from your computer, with detailed reports and automatic calculations to facilitate decision-making.

Moneydance: Moneydance combines simplicity and powerful features for financial tracking. It supports online bank accounts, budget planning, and expense analysis. Its interactive charts make it easy to evaluate your financial situation.

4. **Bank Tools:**

Banking Apps: Almost all banks offer mobile apps that allow you to track account balances, check transaction history, and sometimes classify expenses. Some apps include budgeting features and alerts for significant transactions.

Online Portals: Banks' online portals provide easy and secure access to your financial data. They offer features such as bill management, expense viewing by category, and data export for deeper analysis.

5. **Digital Envelopes:**

Goodbudget: Goodbudget is an app based on the traditional envelope method. It allows you to divide your income into digital envelope categories to track expenses and avoid overspending. It's a great way for those who prefer a visual and segmented approach to financial management.

Mvelopes: Similar to Goodbudget, Mvelopes also uses the envelope budgeting technique. With robust features for expense tracking and budget planning, this app helps maintain financial discipline and achieve goals in an organized manner.

6. **Specialized Tools:**

Spendee: Spendee offers a user-friendly interface for recording and analyzing expenses. It allows you to create shared wallets, ideal for families or roommates who want to track common finances. Graphs and infographics make expense analysis intuitive.

Expensify: Primarily used for business expenses, Expensify is also useful for personal expenses. It allows you to scan receipts, track business mileage, and generate detailed expense reports.

By using these various tools to track expenses and income, you can find the one that best suits your habits and financial needs. Choosing the tool is only part of the equation; it is crucial to use it regularly and systematically to maximize the benefits of your financial tracking efforts.

3.3 Financial Tracking Techniques

To effectively track your finances, it is crucial to adopt techniques that suit your needs and lifestyle. Here are some of the most effective financial tracking techniques to help you keep control over your income and expenses.

1. **Daily Expense Journaling:**

This technique involves recording each expense as soon as it occurs. By immediately noting your purchases and payments, you keep precise and up-to-date tracking of your cash outflows.

- **Mobile App or Notebook:** Use a dedicated mobile app to simplify data entry, or a notebook for those who prefer a paper-based approach.
- **Expense Categories:** Classify each expense according to predefined categories for easy and quick analysis at the end of the month.

2. **Weekly Statement:**

Gather your financial transactions once a week for a more frequent overview of your finances. This technique helps quickly identify irregularities and make real-time adjustments.

- **Account Synchronization:** Connect your bank accounts to a tracking app to automate data collection.
- **Expense Analysis:** Review your weekly transactions and identify categories where you spent more or less than expected.

3. **Automatic Recording:**

Automate the tracking process by using apps and bank tools that automatically record and categorize your transactions.

- **Banks and Apps:** Opt for banks offering integrated tracking features and apps that directly synchronize your financial information.
- **Alerts and Notifications:** Set up alerts to be informed of major transactions or budget limit overruns.

4. **Bank Statement Reconciliation:**

Systematically compare your bank statements with your expense records to ensure data accuracy.
   - **Monthly or Weekly:** Depending on your preference, you can do it monthly or weekly.
   - **Error Correction:** Immediately correct any errors or suspicious transactions spotted during reconciliation.

5. **Using Graphs and Dashboards:**

Visualizing your finances in the form of graphs and dashboards can make analysis more intuitive and quicker.
   - **Financial Apps:** Use apps that provide graphical visualizations of your financial data.
   - **Custom Dashboards:** Create your own dashboards in spreadsheets like Excel or Google Sheets to track important financial indicators.

6. **Envelope Method:**

Allocate a specific amount for each expense category using physical or digital envelopes. This technique limits impulsive spending by forcing you to adhere to predefined limits for each category.
   - **Digital Envelopes:** Use apps that simulate budget envelopes to easily track your expenses.
   - **Physical Envelopes:** Prepare real envelopes containing money reserved for each budget category.

7. **Double-Entry Method:**

Adopt a double-entry accounting system where each transaction is recorded twice: once for the debit (expense) and once for the credit (income or debt reduction).
   - **Accounting Apps:** Use software specifically designed for personal accounting, offering double-entry features.
   - **Accounting Books:** For those who prefer a manual approach, keep a double-entry journal in a dedicated account book.

8. **Tracking Financial Goals:**

Set precise financial goals and regularly track your progress.

- **Goal Segments:** Divide your goals into smaller, trackable segments to measure your progress more detailed and regularly.
- **Regular Reviews:** Schedule regular review sessions to evaluate your progress and adjust your goals or strategies if necessary.

9. **Financial Support Groups:**

Joining or creating support groups where members share their financial progress, challenges, and tips can provide motivation and information benefits.

- **Experience Sharing:** Regular meetings offer a platform to discuss best practices and get constructive feedback.
- **Shared Accountability:** Reporting your progress to a group can reinforce your commitment to tracking and managing your finances.

10. **Personal Financial Audit:**

Periodically conduct personal financial audits to evaluate the effectiveness of your tracking and management techniques.

- **In-Depth Analysis:** Examine your income, expenses, debts, and investments to get a comprehensive view of your financial situation.
- **Audit Report:** Create a personal audit report that summarizes your observations and the corrective actions to take.

By consistently employing these financial tracking techniques, you will have a clear and precise view of your financial situation, allowing you to make informed decisions and stay on track to achieve your financial goals.

3.4 Analyzing and Interpreting Financial Data

Analyzing and interpreting financial data is a crucial step in understanding your financial habits, identifying areas for improvement, and making informed decisions. It transforms raw information into effective strategies and concrete actions to improve your financial situation.

Identifying Trends:

Analyzing financial data helps discern trends and patterns in your income and expenses:

- **Recurring Expenses:** Identify categories where your expenses are consistently high. This may include recurring monthly bills or variable expenses like entertainment.
- **Income Variations:** Detect cycles or seasonal variations in your income, such as annual bonuses or occasional earnings.

Comparing with the Budget:

Comparing your actual expenses and income with the initially planned budget is essential to measure the accuracy of your forecasts and the effectiveness of your management:

- **Budget Discrepancies:** Analyze the discrepancies between the planned budget and actual expenses. Significant discrepancies may indicate forecasting errors or unexpected expenses.
- **Category Adjustment:** Use these comparative data to adjust the amounts allocated to each expense category in your future budget.

Category Expense Analysis:

Dividing expenses by category helps understand where and how your money is spent:

- **Expense Percentage:** Calculate the percentage of your income spent in each category to identify areas that can be reduced.
- **Prioritizing Cuts:** If reductions are necessary, prioritize cuts in non-essential expense categories.

Evaluating Financial Ratios:

Financial ratios are important indicators of your overall financial health:

- **Savings Rate:** The percentage of your income saved each month. A low savings rate may indicate the need to increase savings or reduce expenses.
- **Debt-to-Income Ratio:** The total amount of your debts divided by your income. A high ratio suggests reevaluating the debt repayment approach to avoid over-indebtedness.

Tracking Financial Goals:

Use your data to evaluate your progress towards your short and long-term financial goals:

- **Progress Towards Goals:** Compare your current savings, debt repayments, and investments with the set goals. Adjust your strategies based on the results obtained.
- **Target Dates:** Measure how much you have achieved against the deadlines you set. Delays may require adjusting savings or expenses amounts.

Liquidity Analysis:

Ensure your cash flow is sufficient to cover your current and unexpected expenses:

- **Cash Balance:** Regularly compare your cash balance to the minimum necessary for your monthly expenses and emergency fund.
- **Cash Flow Forecast:** Project your cash inflows and outflows to identify potential periods of cash flow tension.

Investment Evaluation:

Analyzing the performance of your investments helps determine if you are on track to achieve your long-term goals:

- **Investment Returns:** Calculate the return on investment for each asset to assess its performance against expectations.
- **Portfolio Rebalancing:** Periodically reevaluate the allocation of your investments to maintain a balance suited to your risk tolerance and goals.

Interpreting Anomalies:

Anomalies in your financial data may indicate errors or adjustment opportunities:

- **Unusual Transactions:** Look for unusual transactions or entry errors that could distort your analysis.
- **Savings Opportunities:** Identify periods or categories where savings can be achievable, such as unused subscriptions.

Using Graphs and Visualizations:

Graphs and charts can make financial data analysis more accessible and intuitive:

- **Line Graphs:** Use line graphs to visualize trends in your cash flow over time.
- **Pie Charts:** Pie charts show the distribution of expenses by category.
- **Bar Graphs:** Compare monthly or annual expenses side by side to assess variations.

Conclusion and Recommended Actions:

Based on your analysis and interpretation, establish a concrete action plan to improve your financial situation:

- **Immediate Corrective Actions:** Take immediate measures to correct significant discrepancies or identified anomalies.
- **Long-Term Strategies:** Develop long-term strategies to achieve your financial goals, such as increasing your savings rate or diversifying your investments.
- **Continuous Monitoring:** Plan regular financial review sessions to track the evolution of your situation and adjust your plans accordingly.

By applying these analysis and interpretation techniques to the collected financial data, you will be better equipped to navigate the complex landscape of personal financial management and make decisions that promote financial health and the achievement of your economic goals.

3.5 Practical Financial Tracking Case Study

To concretely illustrate financial tracking concepts, let's examine a practical case study. This case study details how a person can track their finances, analyze data, and adjust their budget to achieve their financial goals.

Individual Profile:
- **Name:** Marie
- **Age:** 35 years old
- **Family Status:** Single
- **Profession:** Software Developer
- **Net Monthly Income:** €3,500

Step 1: Collecting Financial Information

Marie starts by gathering all information regarding her income and expenses:

Income:
- Main Salary: €3,500

Fixed Expenses:
- Rent: €1,000
- Home Insurance: €50
- Car Insurance: €80
- Utilities: €150
- Phone/Internet: €50
- Student Loan: €200

Total Fixed Expenses: €1,530

Variable Expenses:
- Groceries: €300
- Transportation (gas): €100
- Entertainment: €150
- Dining Out: €100
- Clothing: €100

- Health and Wellness: €50
- Miscellaneous: €100

Total Variable Expenses: €900

Occasional Expenses:
- Car Repairs: €50
- Gifts: €100
- Medical Expenses: €50

Total Occasional Expenses: €200

Savings and Investments:
- Emergency Fund: €300
- Retirement Savings: €200
- Investments: €200

Total Savings and Investments: €700

Step 2: Daily and Weekly Expense Tracking

Marie uses a financial management app to record each expense. She categorizes all her transactions, giving her a clear and precise view of her daily and weekly expenses.

Step 3: Monthly Financial Data Analysis

At the end of the month, Marie analyzes her data:
- **Total Income:** €3,500
- **Total Expenses:** €1,530 (fixed) + €900 (variable) + €200 (occasional) = €2,630
- **Total Savings and Investments:** €700
- **Available Balance:** €3,500 - €2,630 - €700 = €170

Marie notices she has an available balance of €170.

Step 4: Comparison with the Initial Budget

Marie compares actual expenses with the planned budget and notes discrepancies in some categories:
- **Variable expenses** in entertainment exceeded by €50 compared to the planned €150.
- **Occasional expenses** for gifts exceeded by €50 compared to the planned €100 due to an unexpected birthday party.

Step 5: Adjustments Based on Analysis

Marie decides to adjust her budget for the following month, considering the discrepancies:
- She reduces the entertainment budget by €50 and increases the gifts budget by €50 to prepare for unexpected events.
- She adds a new expense category "Social Events" with a monthly allocation of €100, allowing better anticipation of party and reception expenses.

Adjusted Variable Expense Budget:
- **Entertainment:** €100
- **Social Events:** €100

Step 6: Tracking Financial Goals

Marie ensures that her financial goals align with her actual expenses:
- She continues to save €500 each month for her emergency fund and retirement savings.
- The remaining €170 each month will be split between additional investment projects and specific savings for vacations.

Step 7: Using Graphs to Visualize Data

Marie uses her financial app's graphical features to visualize her data:
- A pie chart shows the distribution of her expenses by category.
- A line graph compares her actual and expected expenses for each ongoing budget category.

Step 8: Action Plan for the Next Month

With the collected and analyzed information, Marie plans the following month:
- She keeps an eye on variable and occasional expense categories to check if the adjustments yield the expected results.
- She plans weekly financial reviews to ensure she follows the new adjusted budget.

Marie's case study demonstrates how to effectively track, analyze, and interpret financial data, leading to precise budget adjustments. This enables proactive and effective management, helping to achieve financial goals while anticipating and adapting to the unexpected.

CHAPTER 4: TOOLS AND APPLICATIONS FOR MONEY MANAGEMENT

Effective financial management requires the use of appropriate tools. In this chapter, we will explore various mobile and online applications that can simplify the management of your personal finances, offering practical ways to track your expenses, plan your budgets, and achieve your financial goals with greater ease.

4.1 Overview of Traditional Tools

Traditional financial management tools remain proven and effective methods for tracking and organizing your personal finances. They offer simplicity and accessibility, making them particularly suitable for those who prefer a manual and tangible approach to money management.

Account Books:

Account books are among the most basic and accessible tools for tracking your finances. They simply consist of a notebook or ledger where you can record all your financial transactions:

- **Simplicity of Use:** All you need is a pen and a notebook to get started. Each expense and income is manually noted, allowing for a clear and orderly view.
- **Customization:** You can organize the book into sections for different types of expenses and income, color-code it as you like, and make it as detailed as necessary.
- **Accessibility:** No need for a computer or internet, making this tool ideal for quick use on the go.

Advantages:

- **Simplicity:** Easy to use without requiring technical skills.
- **Customization:** Allows for personalized and creative financial management.
- **No Internet Needed:** Completely offline, ideal for those who prefer to avoid digital tools.

Disadvantages:

- **Accuracy:** Risk of human error when manually recording transactions.
- **Time-Consuming:** Manual data entry can be time-consuming.
- **Lack of Visualization:** Difficult to generate detailed reports or charts.

Excel Spreadsheets:

Spreadsheets like Excel offer increased flexibility and automated calculation capabilities while remaining relatively simple to use:

- **Data Organization:** Excel allows you to create custom tables to record your expenses, income, and automatically calculate your monthly, weekly, or annual totals.
- **Calculation Functions:** With built-in formulas, you can easily calculate sums, averages, and other important financial statistics, greatly simplifying data analysis.
- **Visualization:** Excel also enables the creation of charts and dashboards for a clear visualization of your financial situation. You can create bar, line, or pie charts to present your data visually and intuitively.

Advantages:
- **Flexibility:** Highly customizable with formulas and macros.
- **Automation:** Allows for automatic calculations and advanced analyses.
- **Visualization:** Ability to create visual charts and dashboards.

Disadvantages:
- **Learning Curve:** Can be complex for those unfamiliar with Excel.
- **Human Error:** Risk of errors if formulas are incorrectly configured.
- **Accessibility:** Requires a computer or mobile app to access.

Accounting Ledgers:

Accounting ledgers resemble account books but with a more structured and detailed approach:

- **Formal Structure:** Accounting ledgers are often pre-printed with columns for dates, transaction descriptions, debit and credit amounts, making it easier to categorize and track transactions.
- **Increased Accuracy:** Commonly used in professional accounting, ledgers help maintain rigorous accuracy in managing your personal finances.

Advantages:
- **Structure:** Pre-printed with columns for organized entry.
- **Accuracy:** Commonly used in professional accounting for their rigor.

Disadvantages:

- **Rigidity:** Less flexibility for customization to your specific needs.
- **Lack of Visualization and Automation:** No capability for advanced analysis or automatic report generation.

Physical Receipt Wallets:

Keeping physical wallets to organize and store your receipts can be useful for expense verification and tax preparation:

- **Systematic Organization:** Sort receipts by expense categories or by period (month, quarter), making them easy to reference later.
- **Proof of Purchase:** Keeping receipts is important for refunds or exchanges and for tax documentation.

Financial Calendars:

Financial calendars help plan and remind you of important financial events such as bill due dates, loan payments, and savings goals:

- **Visual Planning:** Calendars allow you to see important dates at a glance, facilitating cash flow management and anticipating financial needs.
- **Payment Reminders:** By marking payment due dates on the calendar, you avoid missed payments that could lead to late fees or penalties.

Budget Envelopes:

Using physical envelopes to manage your finances is a traditional yet highly effective method for controlling expenses:

- **Precise Allocation:** Place cash in dedicated envelopes for different expense categories (groceries, entertainment, transportation, etc.). Once an envelope's money is spent, no further spending can occur in that category until the next month.
- **Financial Discipline:** This method imposes strict limits on each expense category, making it easier to manage your overall budget.

Personal Finance Journals:

Keeping a personal finance journal adds a reflective dimension

to financial management. Record not only transactions but also financial observations and reflections:
- **Reflection and Analysis:** In addition to recording transactions, you can reflect on your spending habits, note financial challenges encountered, and assess your progress toward financial goals.
- **Comprehensive Documentation:** This journal can serve as a reference document to understand the motivations behind your financial decisions and adapt your strategies accordingly.

Traditional financial management tools still have a place in an increasingly digital world. Their simplicity and accessibility make them valuable options for those seeking a tangible and adaptable approach to managing personal finances. They lay the solid foundation necessary for rigorous financial discipline and increased control over your resources.

4.2 Mobile and Online Applications

Mobile and online applications offer modern and practical solutions for personal financial management. They allow easy tracking of income, expenses, and investments, while providing a range of features for more effective and informed financial management.

Mint:

Mint is one of the most popular financial management apps. It centralizes all your financial information in one place:

- **Account Synchronization:** Connect your bank, credit, loan, and investment accounts for a unified view.
- **Automatic Categorization:** Mint automatically categorizes your transactions, making it easier to track expenses by category.
- **Budgeting:** Create personalized budgets and receive alerts when you approach or exceed your limits.
- **Reports and Analyses:** Detailed graphs and reports provide a clear view of your financial situation and spending habits.

Advantages:

- **Centralization:** All financial information in one place.
- **Automation:** Automatic categorization of transactions.
- **Detailed Reports:** Graphs and analyses for quick financial insights.

Disadvantages:

- **Security and Privacy:** Potential risk associated with connecting multiple financial accounts.
- **Initial Complexity:** May require some time to adapt.

You Need A Budget (YNAB):

YNAB is an app focused on the zero-based budgeting method. It helps users allocate every euro of their income to specific categories before spending:

- **Proactive Allocation:** Plan every euro of your budget to cover current and future expenses.

- **Debt Management:** YNAB offers tools to track and repay debts in an organized manner.
- **Progress Reports:** Track your progress toward financial goals with clear reports and graphs.
- **Integrated Training:** Access online workshops and guides to improve your financial knowledge and practice.

Advantages:
- **Proactive Budgeting:** Encourages planning and proactive allocation of income.
- **Included Training:** Access to workshops and guides to improve financial skills.

Disadvantages:
- **Cost:** Can be more expensive compared to other free apps.
- **Setup Time:** May take time to adapt to the zero-based budgeting method.

PocketGuard:

PocketGuard simplifies money management by showing how much you have left to spend after covering your necessities and savings contributions:
- **"In My Pocket":** A feature that calculates what you have left to spend after accounting for income, expenses, and savings goals.
- **Bank Synchronization:** Securely connect your accounts to automate expense tracking.
- **Alerts and Notifications:** Receive alerts for important expenses, bill payments, and other crucial transactions.
- **Custom Categories:** Create and manage spending categories that fit your lifestyle.

Advantages:
- **Simplicity:** Simplified and easy-to-use interface.
- **Real-Time Tracking:** "In My Pocket" shows how much you have left to spend.

Disadvantages:
- **Limited Customization Options:** Less flexibility compared to some other apps.

- **Limited Advanced Features:** Less suitable for complex financial management.

Goodbudget:

Goodbudget uses the envelope budgeting method but in a digital version:

- **Virtual Envelopes:** Divide your income into virtual envelopes for different budget categories.
- **Multi-Device Sync:** Track your budget across multiple devices, useful for couples and families sharing financial management.
- **Expense Reports:** Analyze your spending habits with detailed reports and graphs.
- **Debt Planning:** Specific tools for planning and tracking debt repayment.

Advantages:

- **Envelope Model:** Helps control spending by specific categories.
- **Sync:** Convenient for couples or families sharing financial management.

Disadvantages:

- **Less Sophisticated Interface:** May seem basic compared to more robust apps.
- **Manual Envelope Management:** Requires regular manual input.

EveryDollar:

EveryDollar is a budgeting app based on the zero-based budgeting method developed by Dave Ramsey:

- **Simplicity:** Simple and intuitive interface to create and track a monthly budget.
- **Bank Connection (Paid Version):** Sync your bank accounts for automatic transaction import.
- **Expense Tracking:** Easily record each expense and track your progress in real time.
- **Mobile and Web:** Available on mobile and web versions for flexible use.

Advantages:
- **Ease of Use:** Intuitive interface for creating and tracking a budget.
- **Practical Orientation:** Based on proven personal finance management principles.

Disadvantages:
- **Limited Free Features:** Some advanced features require a paid subscription.
- **Bank Integration Limited in Free Version:** Account synchronization is paid.

Spendee:

Spendee focuses on personal finance management with a user-friendly and colorful interface:
- **Shared Wallets:** Create shared wallets with family members or roommates to manage common expenses.
- **Data Import:** Import your bank transactions or add them manually.
- **Budgeting:** Set personalized budgets for each spending category.
- **Visual Reports:** Graphs and infographics for visual analysis of your finances.

Advantages:
- **Visual Interface:** Colorful and pleasant interface for tracking finances.
- **Shared Wallets:** Ideal for group financial management.

Disadvantages:
- **Fewer Advanced Tools:** Less advanced financial analysis capabilities compared to other apps.
- **Paid Features:** Some useful features may require a subscription.

Money Manager:

Money Manager offers advanced features for detailed financial management:
- **Recurring Transactions:** Schedule recurring transactions like salaries or loan payments.

- **Report Generation:** Detailed reports by type of expense, category, account, etc.
- **Multi-Device Sync:** Track your finances from multiple devices.
- **Loan and Borrowing Functions:** Track loans given or received and their repayment.

Advantages:
- **Tracks All Transactions:** Scheduling recurring transactions for increased automation.
- **Detailed Financial Management:** Tools to track loans, deposits, and withdrawals.

Disadvantages:
- **Complex Interface:** May not be as easy to use for beginners.
- **Limited Sync:** Sometimes limited to certain devices or platforms.

Personal Capital:

Personal Capital goes beyond simple budgeting by offering robust investment management tools:
- **Overall Financial View:** Connect all your bank and investment accounts for a comprehensive view of your wealth.
- **Investment Management:** Track the performance of your investments with detailed tools.
- **Retirement Planning:** Specific tools to plan your retirement savings and assess if you are on track.
- **Financial Advice:** Access personalized financial advice to optimize your investments.

Advantages:
- **Overall View:** Integration of bank and investment accounts for a complete overview.
- **Investment Tools:** Advanced features for investment management.

Disadvantages:
- **Complexity:** May be too complex for those seeking simple budget management.

- **Investment-Focused:** Less suitable for those focusing solely on budgeting.

Wally:

Wally focuses on internationalization and personal expense management:

- **Budget Options:** Create budgets for different spending groups, savings, and even for travel.
- **Global Tracking:** Ideal for international users with multiple currency support.
- **Receipt Scanner:** Scan receipts for quick and accurate expense entry.
- **Family Sharing:** Features to share budgets and track family expenses.

Advantages:

- **International Adaptability:** Supports multiple currencies, ideal for international users.
- **Receipt Scanner:** Convenient feature for quickly recording expenses.

Disadvantages:

- **User Interface:** May not be as intuitive as some other apps.
- **Fewer Advanced Features:** Less sophisticated analysis capabilities.

Creating and maintaining an accurate budget, tracking expenses in real time, and analyzing financial habits are made easier with these applications. They provide a combination of ease of use and advanced features, allowing you to manage your personal finances effectively and intuitively. By integrating these tools into your financial routine, you can improve transparency, management, and optimization of your money.

4.3 Choosing the Right Tools According to Your Needs

Choosing financial management tools should be informed by a clear understanding of your personal needs and financial goals. Here's how to determine the best tools suited to different situations and lifestyles.

For Budgeting Beginners:

Recommended Tools:

- **Account Books:** The simplicity of this tool makes it a great option for those starting to track their finances.
- **Goodbudget:** The envelope budgeting approach helps beginners master expense control.

Desired Features:

- **Ease of Use:** The tool should be simple and intuitive to avoid frustration.
- **Educational Support:** Tools that offer guides or tutorials can help better understand the basics of financial management.

For Those Who Want to Track Every Euro:

Recommended Tools:

- **You Need A Budget (YNAB):** The proactive budgeting method helps allocate every euro before spending.
- **PocketGuard:** Offers real-time tracking and shows how much you have left to spend after covering necessities and savings contributions.

Desired Features:

- **Detailed Categorization:** The tool should allow precise classification of expenses.
- **Real-Time Tracking:** Real-time updates help track exactly where every euro goes.

For Families or Groups:

Recommended Tools:

- **Goodbudget:** Compatible with multiple users, ideal for couples and families.

- **Spendee:** Allows the creation of shared wallets to manage common expenses.

Desired Features:

- **Multi-Device Sync:** Important for all group members to access and update the budget.
- **Data Sharing:** Features that allow easy sharing of financial data with other members.

For Professionals with Multiple Jobs:

Recommended Tools:

- **Mint:** Centralizes financial information from multiple accounts and jobs in one place.
- **Money Manager:** Offers detailed tracking of transactions and income from different sources.

Desired Features:

- **Multi-Account Management:** The tool should manage multiple accounts and income sources efficiently.
- **Automated Entries:** The ability to automatically import transactions from various sources simplifies management.

For Those with Advanced Financial Management Skills:

Recommended Tools:

- **Excel:** Allows maximum customization with formulas and macros.
- **Personal Capital:** Robust tools for investment management in addition to budgeting.

Desired Features:

- **Advanced Analysis:** Tools offering sophisticated analysis and visualization capabilities.
- **Customization:** Allows creating custom tables and charts for specific analyses.

For Those Looking to Reduce Debt:

Recommended Tools:

- **You Need A Budget (YNAB):** Designed to help repay debts in an organized manner.
- **EveryDollar:** Focused on personal finance management principles to avoid debt.

Desired Features:
- **Debt Planning:** Specific features to track and plan debt repayment.
- **Progress Tracking:** Ability to generate detailed reports on debt repayment progress.

For International Users:

Recommended Tools:
- **Wally:** Multiple currency support, ideal for frequent travelers.
- **Spendee:** Also suitable for multi-currency management and shared wallets.

Desired Features:
- **Multi-Currency Support:** Important to track finances in different currencies.
- **Global Accessibility:** The tool should be accessible and usable wherever you go.

For Active Investors:

Recommended Tools:
- **Personal Capital:** Advanced tools to track and manage investments.
- **Quicken:** In addition to budgeting, offers comprehensive investment management features.

Desired Features:
- **Investment Analysis:** Features to analyze investment performance.
- **Portfolio Rebalancing:** Capabilities to assist in regular portfolio rebalancing.

By choosing tools tailored to your specific needs, you optimize the management of your personal finances. Whether you are a beginner, family member, professional with multiple income sources, or active investor, there are tools designed to help you achieve your financial goals efficiently and structured.

4.5 Security of Online Financial Data

With the rise in popularity of mobile apps and online tools for financial management, the security of personal and financial data has become a major concern. Protecting your sensitive information is essential to prevent fraud and identity theft. Here are the main measures and practices to ensure the security of your online financial data.

Using Strong Passwords:

A strong password is the first line of defense against intrusions:

- **Complexity:** Use complex passwords consisting of uppercase and lowercase letters, numbers, and symbols.
- **Unique:** Each account should have a unique password to prevent one compromised password from affecting multiple accounts.
- **Regular Renewal:** Change your passwords periodically to enhance security.

Two-Factor Authentication (2FA):

Two-factor authentication adds an extra layer of security:

- **One-Time Codes:** In addition to the password, a unique code sent via SMS or generated by an authentication app is required to access your accounts.
- **Biometrics:** Using facial recognition or fingerprints on compatible devices adds biometric security.

Securing Devices:

Ensure the devices used to access your financial data are secure:

- **Regular Updates:** Keep your operating systems and applications up to date with the latest security updates.
- **Anti-Virus:** Use anti-virus and anti-malware software to protect against online threats.
- **Device Locking:** Use passwords, PINs, or biometric data to lock your devices.

Using Secure Connections:

Access your financial accounts only via secure connections:

- **HTTPS:** Ensure financial websites use the HTTPS protocol, which encrypts data transmitted between your browser and the website.
- **Secure Wi-Fi:** Avoid accessing your financial accounts over public Wi-Fi networks. Use private and secure networks or a VPN (Virtual Private Network) for an extra layer of protection.

Monitoring and Alerts:

Enable alerts to monitor any suspicious activity on your accounts:
- **Instant Notifications:** Set up notifications for unusual transactions or login attempts from unrecognized devices.
- **Regular Review:** Regularly check your transaction history to identify any unauthorized activity.

Using Trusted Applications:

Download and use only reputable and reliable financial management apps:
- **Preliminary Research:** Check reviews, ratings, and the developers' background before downloading a new app.
- **Official Sites:** Download apps only from official app stores (App Store, Google Play).

Protecting Personal Information:

Be vigilant about the personal information you share online:
- **Phishing:** Beware of suspicious emails, links, or attachments that may try to collect your personal data.
- **Digital Identity:** Never share your passwords or login information with anyone. Be cautious with the information you share on social networks.

Data Encryption:

Sensitive data should be encrypted to prevent it from being intercepted and used maliciously:
- **Device Encryption:** Use encryption to secure data stored on your mobile devices and computers.
- **Transmission Encryption:** Ensure communications between your devices and financial app servers are encrypted.

Regular Backups:

Regularly back up your financial data to prevent loss:
- **Secure Cloud:** Use secure cloud storage services to back up your financial information.
- **Local Storage:** Keep encrypted backup copies on secure external hard drives.

Caution with App Permissions:

Pay attention to the permissions you grant to mobile applications:
- **Minimal Permissions:** Only grant necessary permissions for the app to function.
- **Frequent Reviews:** Regularly check the permissions granted to apps and revoke those no longer needed.

Documentation and Access Tracking:

Keep track of granted access and changes made to your accounts:
- **Access Logs:** Use access logs to track all logins to your financial accounts.
- **Change History:** Keep a history of major changes made to your security settings.

By applying these security measures, you can protect your financial data against online threats and ensure your sensitive information is secure. Constant vigilance and adherence to best security practices are essential for safe and effective online personal financial management.

CHAPTER 5: ADOPTING POSITIVE FINANCIAL BEHAVIOR

Understanding financial behavior is essential to mastering and adhering to a budget. This final chapter will help you identify and overcome behavioral biases while developing positive financial habits. You will learn to adopt a more thoughtful and disciplined approach for optimal and sustainable financial management.

5.1. Introduction to Financial Behavior

The Importance of Psychology in Financial Management

Managing personal finances is not just about numbers and calculations. In reality, a significant part of our financial success depends on our behavior and money habits. Financial psychology, which studies how our emotions and perceptions influence our financial decisions, plays a crucial role in our ability to effectively manage our budget.

The financial decisions we make daily are often influenced by cognitive and emotional biases. For example, feelings of overconfidence can lead us to underestimate our expenses or overestimate our ability to repay debts. Similarly, emotions such as fear or stress can lead to impulsive decisions, like buying non-essential items for comfort.

Understanding these psychological influences allows us to become aware of potential pitfalls and develop strategies to avoid them. By adopting healthy financial behaviors and integrating thoughtful practices into our daily management, we can not only master our budget but also achieve our financial goals more efficiently and sustainably.

Chapter Objectives

This chapter aims to help readers adopt positive financial behavior to master and adhere to their budget. We will explore the main behavioral biases that can hinder healthy financial management and propose strategies to develop positive financial habits. Finally, we will discuss specific techniques for tracking and adjusting your budget, as well as tools and applications that can facilitate this process.

By understanding and mastering the psychological aspects of financial management, you will be better equipped to make informed decisions, avoid common pitfalls, and implement sustainable practices that will help you stay true to your budget.

Whether you are new to financial management or looking to improve your existing skills, this chapter will provide the knowledge and tools necessary for success.

5.2 Understanding Behavioral Biases

Explanations

Behavioral biases are cognitive tendencies that influence the way we make decisions, often unconsciously. In financial management, these biases can lead us to make decisions that are not always rational or optimal. Understanding these biases is the first step to overcoming them and improving our financial behavior.

Overconfidence Bias

Overconfidence bias occurs when we overestimate our knowledge, skills, or ability to predict the future. In finance, this can lead to reckless decisions, such as investing in risky stocks without sufficient research or ignoring warnings of excessive spending.

Example: An individual may believe they can predict stock market movements better than experts and therefore invest heavily in speculative stocks, potentially leading to significant financial losses.

How to overcome it: Recognize that uncertainty is an integral part of financial decisions and strive to make choices based on thorough research and expert advice.

Loss Aversion Bias

Loss aversion is our tendency to prefer avoiding losses over making equivalent gains. This bias can make us overly cautious, preventing us from making beneficial financial decisions, or lead us to hold onto losing investments out of fear of realizing a loss.

Example: An investor may hesitate to sell a declining stock to avoid realizing a loss, even if holding onto the investment is contrary to their long-term financial interests.

How to overcome it: Focus on long-term financial goals and evaluate investment decisions rationally, considering data and trends rather than emotions.

Anchoring and Status Quo Bias

Anchoring occurs when we rely too heavily on the first information received (the anchor) to make decisions. Status quo bias is our tendency to prefer the current situation and avoid change, even when change would be beneficial.

Example: When setting a budget, a person may base it on past expenses without seeking to adjust or optimize them, even if their needs and goals have changed.

How to overcome it: Regularly review your finances and be open to necessary adjustments based on new information and changes in personal or economic circumstances.

The Impact of These Biases on Budget Management

These behavioral biases can seriously hinder our ability to establish and adhere to a budget. For example:

- **Overconfidence:** Can lead to excessive spending or reckless investments, exceeding the planned budget.
- **Loss Aversion:** Can prevent necessary financial decisions, such as reallocating funds or cutting non-essential expenses.
- **Anchoring and Status Quo:** Can maintain inefficient spending habits and prevent adapting the budget to changes in income or priorities.

By becoming aware of these biases and adopting strategies to manage them, you can improve your budgeting discipline, make wiser financial decisions, and achieve your financial goals more effectively.

5.3 Strategies for Developing Positive Financial Habits

Setting Realistic Budget Goals

The first step to adopting good financial behavior is to set clear and realistic budget goals. These goals should be Specific, Measurable, Achievable, Relevant, and Time-bound (SMART).

Example:
- **Specific Goal:** "Save €500 for an emergency fund by the end of the year."
- **Measurable Goal:** "Set aside €50 each month."
- **Achievable Goal:** Ensure this goal is realistic based on your current income and expenses.
- **Relevant Goal:** An emergency fund is essential for financial stability.
- **Time-bound Goal:** Deadline by the end of the year.

By setting such goals, you create a clear roadmap that guides your financial decisions and motivates you to stay disciplined.

Creating Healthy Financial Routines

Healthy financial routines are regular habits that facilitate managing your finances and help you stay on budget. Here are some practices to adopt:

Monthly Financial Review:
- Review your income, expenses, and savings each month.
- Compare actual expenses to the planned budget.
- Identify discrepancies and adjust the budget if necessary.

Automatic Savings:
- Set up automatic transfers from your checking account to a savings account each payday.
- This ensures that saving is prioritized before discretionary spending.

Daily Expense Tracking:
- Use a financial management app to record and categorize

each expense.
- This helps you keep an accurate track of your spending habits and identify areas where you can save.

Techniques to Avoid Impulsive Spending

Impulsive spending can easily derail your budget. Here are some techniques to avoid it:

Shopping List:
- Make a list before going shopping and stick to it.
- This reduces unplanned purchases and helps you stay on budget.

24-Hour Rule:
- If you are considering a non-essential purchase, wait 24 hours before making it.
- This gives you time to think and decide if the purchase is really necessary.

Limiting Exposure to Temptations:
- Avoid browsing shopping websites or visiting stores without a specific buying intention.
- Unsubscribe from promotional newsletters and notifications.

The Importance of Continuous Financial Education

Financial management is a skill that improves with time and continuous learning. Here are some ways to continue educating yourself:

Readings and Resources:
- Read books and articles on personal financial management.
- Follow blogs and podcasts specializing in personal finance.

Workshops and Training:
- Attend workshops and seminars on financial management.
- Consider online courses on specific financial topics.

Consultation with Experts:
- Consult a financial advisor for personalized advice.
- Take advantage of free consultations often offered by banks and financial institutions.

By adopting these strategies, you can develop positive financial habits that will help you master and adhere to your budget. The key is consistency and commitment to your financial goals, while remaining flexible and ready to adjust your plan as needed.

5.4 Techniques to Stick to Your Budget

Regular Expense Tracking

To stick to a budget, it is essential to regularly track your expenses. This allows you to know exactly where your money is going and quickly identify deviations from your initial budget.

Tracking Methods:

- **Mobile Apps:** Use apps like Mint, YNAB, or PocketGuard to automatically track your expenses. These apps can sync your bank accounts and categorize your transactions.
- **Spreadsheets:** If you prefer a manual approach, use spreadsheets like Excel or Google Sheets. Create tables to record your income and expenses, and update them regularly.
- **Account Books:** For those who prefer a more traditional method, keeping an account book can be effective. Note each expense as it occurs and categorize them.

Tracking Frequency:

- **Daily:** Record your expenses each day to avoid accumulating many transactions at the end of the month.
- **Weekly:** Review your weekly expenses and compare them to your budget.
- **Monthly:** Conduct an end-of-month review to analyze your spending habits and adjust your budget if necessary.

Budget Adjustment and Revision

A budget is not fixed; it must be flexible and adaptable to your changing needs and circumstances.

Gap Analysis:

- Compare your actual expenses to those planned in your budget.
- Identify categories where you exceeded the budget and those where you under-spent.

Adjustments:

- If you regularly exceed the budget in a category, increase

- the allocation for that category and reduce another less prioritized one.
- If you have unforeseen expenses, adjust your budget to integrate them without unbalancing your finances.

Periodic Revisions:
- Review your budget monthly to account for income and expense variations.
- Adjust your financial goals based on changes in your situation, such as a salary increase or a new recurring expense.

Using Financial Management Tools and Applications

Financial management tools and applications can greatly facilitate sticking to your budget by automating tracking and providing detailed analyses (refer to Chapter 4).

Establishing Control Mechanisms

To ensure you stick to your budget, it is useful to establish control mechanisms.

Envelope Budgeting:
- Use physical envelopes or digital envelopes to divide your money into different expense categories.
- Once an envelope's money is exhausted, avoid further spending in that category until the next month.

Separate Bank Accounts:
- Create separate bank accounts for different expense categories, such as bills, savings, and entertainment.
- This helps you easily visualize how much money is available for each type of expense.

Limiting Credit Card Use:
- Mainly use debit cards or cash to avoid spending money you don't have.
- If you use credit cards, make sure to pay off the full balance each month to avoid interest.

By adopting these techniques, you can not only create a realistic budget but also adhere to it consistently. The key is discipline and consistency in tracking and adjusting your finances, using the tools and strategies that best suit your lifestyle and financial needs.

CONCLUSION

Personal financial management is an essential skill that deeply influences all aspects of our lives. By understanding the basics of financial management and adopting solid budgeting practices, you can take control of your finances, prevent unnecessary debt, and achieve your economic goals.

Establishing a realistic budget and rigorously following it helps maintain a balance between income and expenses while promoting savings and investment. The effective use of modern tools, whether traditional or digital, makes this process more accessible and efficient. By regularly analyzing your financial data and adjusting your strategies as needed, you continuously improve your financial situation.

The chapter on financial behavior highlighted the importance of understanding and managing the behavioral biases that can affect our financial decisions. By adopting positive financial habits and being aware of psychological influences, you will be better equipped to maintain a balanced budget and achieve your financial goals sustainably.

Choosing the right tools according to your needs and ensuring the security of your financial data is crucial in an increasingly digital world. Whether you are a beginner or an expert in financial management, there are solutions tailored to each profile that will help you navigate your financial journey with confidence and assurance.

Your journey towards better financial management is a continuous process that requires perseverance and discipline. By applying the principles and techniques shared in this guide, you can build a solid foundation for your financial future. Take the time to regularly reassess your progress, celebrate your successes, and adjust your plans to overcome challenges. With solid knowledge and appropriate tools, you are well-equipped to achieve your goals and live a financially stable and fulfilling life.

If this guide has been helpful to you, I encourage you to leave a rating and a comment. Your feedback is valuable and will help other readers discover and benefit from this book. Thank you for your trust and happy financial management!

www.ingramcontent.com/pod-product-compliance
Lightning Source LLC
Chambersburg PA
CBHW071951210526
45479CB00003B/897